TABLE OF CONTENTS

LETTER FROM SLNP ART

SLNP Gallery Share Love n Peace
Chicago's talent is like a hidden gem waiting to shine. Let's bring the spotlight to the rising stars of the Windy City and watch them light up the world.

Chicago is on the verge of a creative revolution, and we're thrilled to introduce you to the rising stars reshaping our city's cultural landscape. From musicians crafting groundbreaking sounds to podcasters igniting conversations, videographers capturing the city's essence, gaming streamers redefining entertainment, and brand ambassadors amplifying our identity, Chicago's talent pool is boundless.

In every chord, frame, and pixel, our city's vibrancy shines through. We're committed to showcasing these talents' exceptional journeys, inspirations, and projects. Join us in celebrating the burgeoning creative energy that's propelling Chicago into a new era of cultural innovation.

If you know of local talents deserving recognition or have stories to share, don't hesitate to reach out. Let's unite in fostering a thriving creative community that continues to enrich Chicago's cultural fabric.

SNPArt

Editor-in-Chief

SLNP GALLERY

Exciting news from Chi-Town! Introducing "SLNP Gallery Share Love & Peace," Stay tuned for stylish designs that spread positivity and unity. Let's all share love and peace together through fashion! #ShareLoveNPeace Chicago

INTRODUCING REHNBOWZ: THE MULTIFACETED CREATIVE SENSATION OF CHICAGO

Chicago is about to witness a creative whirlwind like never before, and at the heart of it all is the dynamic talent known as Rehnbowz. This budding photographer and music artist is making waves in the Windy City's art and music scene, promising a fresh and vibrant perspective that's impossible to ignore.

Rehnbowz is a name that stands out, just like her work. As a photographer, her lens captures the vivid and diverse tapestry of Chicago's urban landscape, focusing on the city's vibrant colors, cultures, and characters. Each shot is a burst of life and energy, revealing Rehnbowz's unique ability to showcase the beauty in everyday moments.

REHNBOWZ IN CHICAGO

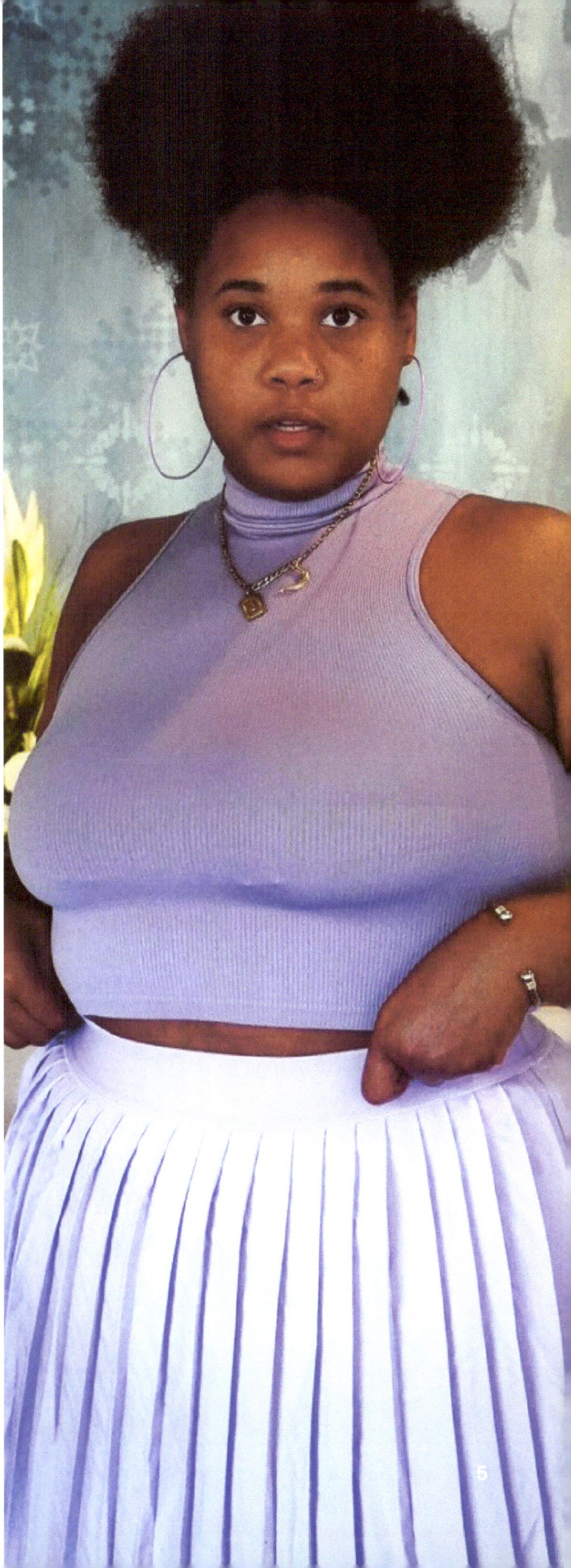

But Rehnbowz doesn't stop at photography. This multifaceted artist also delves into music, crafting a blend of Afro Pop, R&B Soul, and House that is nothing short of electrifying. Her music is a sonic journey that mirrors her photographic storytelling, evoking a sense of emotion and groove that keeps listeners hooked.

Rehnbowz's Afro Pop tracks are an infectious blend of rhythms that transport you straight to the heart of Africa, while her R&B Soul ballads tug at your heartstrings with soulful vocals and poetic lyrics. And when it's time to dance, her House music beats will have you moving all night long. With Rehnbowz, you get a full-sensory experience that's as diverse as Chicago itself.

Chicago, get ready to immerse yourself in the mesmerizing world of Rehnbowz. As a photographer and music artist, she is set to redefine your perception of creativity, offering a kaleidoscope of colors, sounds, and emotions that will leave an indelible mark on the city's cultural landscape. Don't miss the chance to witness this rising star in action, as Rehnbowz paints Chicago with her unique artistic vision and sound. It's a journey you won't want to miss.

NIQUE'S & NOTTS CREATIONS

Dreams Come to Life: Nique's & Notts Creations - Illinois Premier Event Magic Makers!

Niquesnottscreations@gmail.com | (815)-549-5087

In the bustling heart of Illinois, an event planning dynamo by the name of Dominique is making waves with her extraordinary venture, "Nique's & Notts Creations." Her passion and talent for orchestrating the most magical moments imaginable have elevated her to the status of Illinois' go-to event planner. From the sweetness of baby showers to the grandeur of weddings and everything in between, Nique is the mastermind behind countless unforgettable occasions.

Nique's expertise lies in her ability to transform ordinary gatherings into unforgettable memories. Her baby showers are nothing short of enchanting, with themes that bring parents' dreams to life. From whimsical woodland wonderlands to elegant gender reveals, Nique's & Notts Creations infuses each celebration with creativity and care.

For birthdays, Nique's touch adds a dash of wonder and whimsy that captivates guests of all ages. Whether it's a child's first milestone or a milestone birthday, her eye for detail and penchant for innovative themes make each event a unique and memorable experience.

However, where Nique truly shines is in the realm of weddings. As couples embark on their lifelong journey together, Nique ensures that their special day is an unparalleled reflection of their love story. With meticulous planning and an extensive network of trusted vendors, she crafts weddings that are nothing short of fairy tales.

Nique's & Notts Creations is not just an event planning company; it's an embodiment of creativity, dedication, and personalized service. Nique's unwavering commitment to her clients, combined with her impeccable taste and attention to detail, has made her an indispensable asset to those seeking to turn their dreams into reality.

In a world where every occasion deserves to be celebrated uniquely, Nique's & Notts Creations is the guiding light that turns visions into vivid realities. Whether it's a joyous baby shower, a spectacular birthday bash, or a breathtaking wedding, Nique's touch ensures that every moment is etched in the hearts of those who experience it. Illinois has found its event planning maestro in Nique, and her magical touch is poised to leave a lasting mark on the events landscape for years to come.

IN DEPTH: QVEEN JOURNEY

CHICAGO, GET READY TO JOURNEY WITH QVEEN

In the vibrant cityscape of Chicago, the name Qveen Journey is fast becoming synonymous with entrepreneurship, mentorship, and cutting-edge fashion design. A dynamic force to be reckoned with, she's set to redefine the city's business landscape while simultaneously leaving her mark on the fashion world.

Qveen Journey's design aesthetic is nothing short of visionary. Her dresses are exquisite works of art, each a testament to her creativity and unwavering commitment to excellence. Beyond her talents as a dress designer, she is a dedicated mentor. She has made it her mission to empower aspiring entrepreneurs, sharing her knowledge and experiences to help others achieve their business dreams. Her mentorship extends not only to fashion designers but also to a diverse range of ambitious individuals eager to carve their paths in the world of business. Qveen Journey's commitment to fostering talent is a testament to her genuine desire to uplift those around her.

Qveen Journey's journey is marked by resilience, creativity, and an unwavering belief in the power of dreams. As she continues to make her mark on both the business and fashion worlds, Chicago finds itself at the epicenter of a transformative force. Her vision extends far beyond city limits, and she's poised to inspire and uplift individuals across the globe, empowering them to pursue their passions and achieve their goals.

Chicago, get ready to embark on a journey of innovation, empowerment, and stunning fashion. Qveen Journey is a testament to the limitless potential of combining business knowledge with creative flair, and her impact on the Windy City is undeniable. As she continues to mentor and design, her influence will undoubtedly shape the future of both fashion and entrepreneurship in Chicago and beyond.

Let Me Rant Podcast

By: Kristy Parque

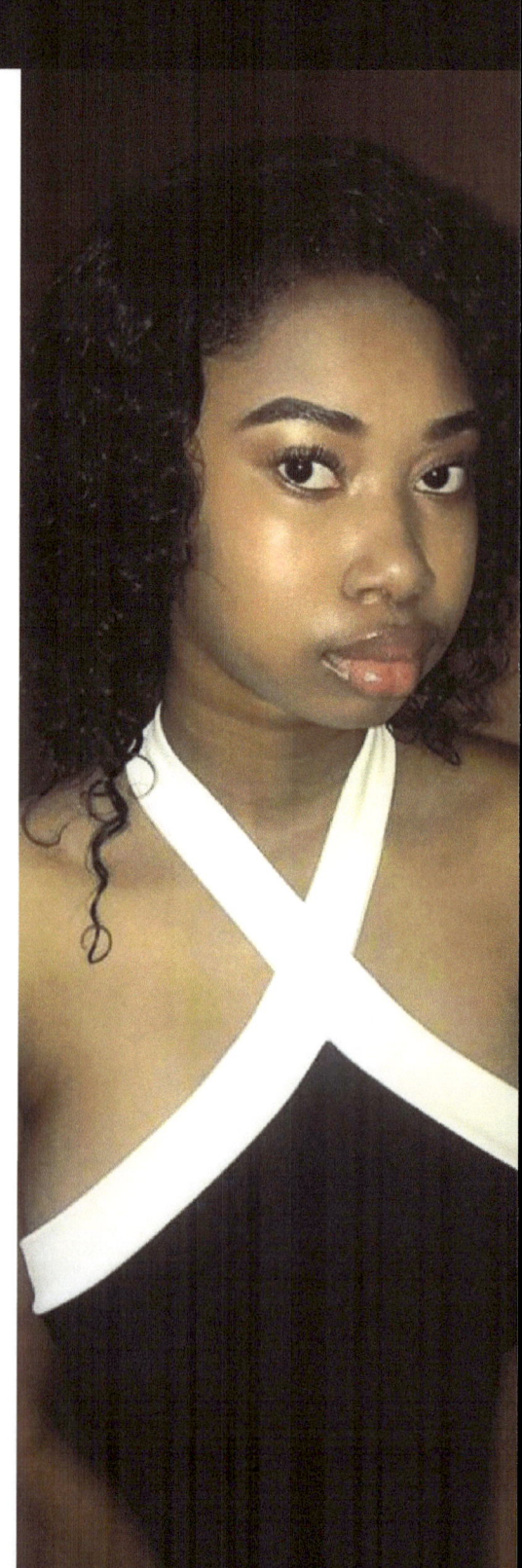

WHO IS KRISTY PARQUE?

I graduated from Valparaiso University in 2019 with a BA in Creative Writing & Cinema Media Studies. While I was at Valpo, I took many courses on filmmaking and script creation. My specialities are videography, lighting, screenwriting, and more. When I was at Valpo. I was a mentor in the S.M.A.R.T Mentoring Program. I mentored incoming students to maintain the retention rate of students of various cultural backgrounds. My tasks were meeting with my mentee every other week to discuss school, to give advice, and to inform them of resources that would be helpful to their success at Valpo. Also, I was a member of BSO and a desk attendant at Beacon Hall.

In 2019, I was an intern at Salem Baptist Church in their Yellow Door Project program. I was a writer and assistant director for their 2019 Christmas play. The Christmas program was televised on WJYS and it was about four stories that highlighted people from different age ranges and how their life experiences brought hope for Christmas. The purpose of the project was to appeal to various age groups with stories that were inspirational and relatable. Some of the responsibilities that I had were writing a scene, being an assistant director, scouting actors, and facilitating rehearsals. Currently I am an academic counselor.
Let me Rant was an idea that I came up with during the Covid 19 shutdown. I was tired of not being able to go anywhere, so I started the podcast to talk about different topics. Let Me Rant is my everything podcast where I interview people from art backgrounds, business owners and people who make significant impacts on the community. I will be launching a video version and short films as well.
Scan the QR code to listen to my podcast.

AR & VR's impacts on professionals is that they are making technology more advanced and diverse. VR & AR can help to enhance the creativity & acknowledgement of professionals like stock photographers, tv producers and more.

Reference
MIU (2023, 19 June) How AR and VR are Transforming the Future of Businesses
How AR and VR are Transforming the Future of Businesses - MIU Your Creative Digital Agency Digital

VR & AR can help to provide more options for professionals in this industry to advertise their content & receive more feedback from their customer base. Digital Agency Network (2023) says,"AR/VR headsets offer an unprecedented level of immersion, allowing users to step into virtual worlds or overlay digital content onto the real world.(Digital Agency Network,2023)". People can attend concerts, watch movies and do so much more with VR devices. AR & BR have opened up a world of opportunities for media and entertainment professionals to release their products.

AR/VR provide a higher engagement level for stock photographers, TV producers, and research development because it increases the viewing options, it can be used anywhere, and makes enhances consumer interest/connection to various products.

The benefits for the companies or organizations that are investing in these technologies is that it makes content more creative & provides a broader approach. This affirms that companies will have a plethora of benefits from using AR & VR such as a more detailed experience for their customers and saving time on producing products.

Retail companies benefit from using AR & VR because it shows customers a 3D model of the store and helps them to expand their customer base. Customers can use AR to try on outfits and jewelry which can enhance the amount of money in online sales. This can help companies to provide customers with an immersive experience that is convenient and beneficial for both parties.

AR & VR can help to shape the makeup of businesses in the future by making businesses go completely digital and be used as a marketing technique. AR & VR can help businesses to expand their target audiences to reach a larger customer base that is more open-minded regarding innovative technology. Also, businesses can help to make customer experiences more immersive & interesting. VR & AR can help virtual events to be able to be used as a convenience to save money & time that can be implemented in revamping other products.

11

HERE COMES THE
HOME BAKER

Sweet Sensations Await: Chicago's Upcoming Home Baker, 'The Delightful Infusionz'

I In the heart of Chicago, a burgeoning talent is setting the city's taste buds ablaze with a touch of homemade magic. 'The Delightful Infusionz' is the name on everyone's lips, and their delectable creations are proof that Chicago's home baking scene is evolving in exciting ways.

The Delightful Infusionz doesn't just bake; they orchestrate a symphony of flavors that dance on the taste buds. From decadent salt caramel fudge chocolate truffle icecream to KitKat M&M cake with chocolate ganache filling, every bite tells a story of creativity and culinary craftsmanship. Their ability to infuse unexpected ingredients, creating harmonious flavor profiles, is what sets them apart in Chicago's competitive baking scene.

The secret ingredient in every delightful creation? Love and care. 'The Delightful Infusionz' pours their heart into each bake, ensuring that every customer experiences the warmth and comfort of homemade goodness. From the careful selection of ingredients to the meticulous attention to detail, their dedication shines through in every delectable morsel.

Chicago's home baking scene is taking on a fresh, flavorful identity, and 'The Delightful Infusionz' is leading the charge. Their delectable offerings are more than just treats; they are a testament to the power of passion, creativity, and a dash of homemade magic. As they continues to redefine the city's sweet landscape, Chicagoans can look forward to a future filled with delicious surprises and a dash of culinary wonder.

SHONDO REACTS

MEET THE HILARIOUS YOUTUBER REDEFINING REACTION VIDEOS!

SHONDO REACTS: CHICAGO'S COMEDY SENSATION ON YOUTUBE

In the heart of Chicago's vibrant online entertainment scene, a rising star is making waves, and their name is 'Shondo Reacts.' With an infectious sense of humor and a knack for crafting funny reaction videos, Shondo is quickly becoming a household name among YouTube aficionados in Chicago and beyond.

.

Shondo Reacts is not your typical YouTuber. His channel is a comedic goldmine, where they react to a wide array of videos, sharing their witty commentary and infectious laughter. From viral internet sensations to classic movie scenes, Shondo's reactions are a hilarious journey into the world of pop culture.

As Shondo Reacts continues to tickle funny bones and amass a growing legion of fans, Chicago couldn't be prouder to call him one of its own. In a world that often feels too serious, Shondo's ability to make us laugh is a testament to the power of humor and the impact of content creators in our lives. Chicago, get ready to keep laughing with Shondo Reacts because this rising star is bound for even greater comedic heights, and we're all invited along for the hilariously entertaining ride.

SLNP THE EMPIRE

Chicago's Sonic Reign: SLNP The Empire
Takes the Music Scene by Storm

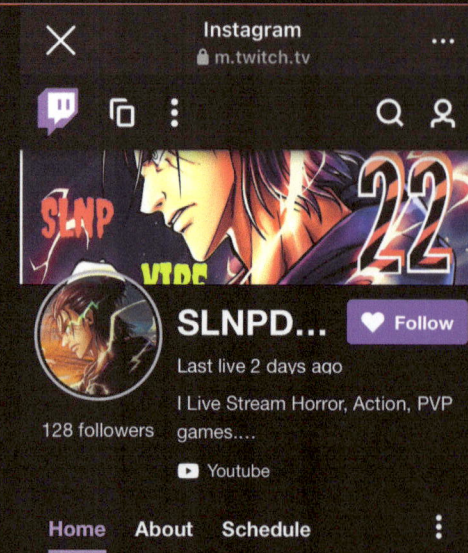

SLNP THE EMPIRE 1.5
SLNP CLXUDZ X SLNP K3Y

SLNP THE EMPIRE
SLNP CLXUDZ X SLNP K3Y X
MELO

SLNP DANTE
YOUTUBE/TWITCH

THANK YOU FOR TAKING THE TIME TO READ OUR MAGAZINE! WE
APPRECIATE YOUR SUPPORT AND HOPE YOU FOUND OUR CONTENT
ENGAGING AND INFORMATIVE. STAY TUNED FOR MORE EXCITING
ARTICLES, STORIES, AND FEATURES IN THE FUTURE. YOUR READERSHIP
MEANS THE WORLD TO US!

–SLNP ART

Advertisement

Advertisement

ADVERTISE WITH SLNP UNSIGNED

SLNP UNSIGNED

09/22
ISSUE 01

GALLERY